The Adventures of Scuba Jack
Copyright 2021 by Beth Costanzo
All rights reserved

Rhinoceros, also called Rhino, is one of the biggest creatures in the world! Our planet has 5 species of rhinoceros - the black rhino and white rhino, that live in Africa, and the Sumatran, Javan, and Indian rhino, that live in the tropical forests and swamps of Asia.

These beasts are known for their giant horns that grow from their snouts. Javan and Indian rhinos have one horn and the white, black and Sumatran rhinos have two.

The largest rhino is the white rhino, which can grow to almost 6 feet tall and weigh around 5,500 pounds! That's the weight of 30 men! Rhinos are herbivores and like to eat tons of grass and plants at night, dawn and dusk. During hot days, rhinos will sleep in the shade or go in muddy pools to cool off. Mud protects their skin from the strong sun and helps keep away bugs.

Rhinoceros usually like to avoid each other except the white rhino may live in a group, called crash. Crashes are usually made up of a female and her calves, but sometimes adult females, called cows, can be together too. Males, called bulls, like to be left alone.

Rhinos spend a lot of time with Oxpeckers on their back, that live off of the parasite insects living in the rhino's thick skin. The bird also alerts the rhino if danger is near. Rhinos have no natural predators, but these beasts get scared easily. Whenever they feel threatened, they charge at it, even if it is harmless. Sadly, there are only 29,000 rhinos left in the wild.

10 Fun Facts
ABOUT RHINO

- There are 5 species of Rhino, two Africans and three Asian.

- White rhinos are the largest, weighing up to 3,500kg.

- Black and white Rhinos are both, in fact, grey.

- Their horn is made from the same stuff as our fingernails.

- Rhinos have poor vision, they mainly rely on their strong sense of smell.

- They communicate through honks, sneezes…and poo.

- A group of rhinos is known as a herd, or a crash.

- Asian rhinos are also excellent swimmers, crossing rivers with ease.

- The white Rhino's horn can grow 7cm every year and the record length is 150cm long!

- Rhinos are speed machines! Running at 30-40 miles per hour, be sure to move out of their way fast.

Rhino QUIZ

Write the correct answer in the box

What are male rhinos called?

1- Bulls

2- Cows

3- Cubs

Write the correct answer in the box

What is a group of rhinos called?

1- Herd

2- Crash

3- Flock

Write the correct answer in the box

What helps to protect a rhino's skin from the sun?

1- Mud

2- Leaves

3- Food

Write the correct answer in the box

What is the largest species of rhino?

1- Indian Rhino

2- Black Rhino

3- White Rhino

Rhino Activities

Tracing Practice

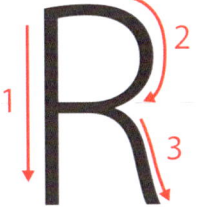 

Trace then rewrite the phrase below.

COUTING PRATICE

2 1 3 5   2 3 4 1

1 3 4 2   5 3 4 2

Count the rhinos then circle the answer.

5 6 7	6 7 8
10 9 11	10 9 8

Maze

Help the Rhino to find its way

COLORING PAGE

CRAFT

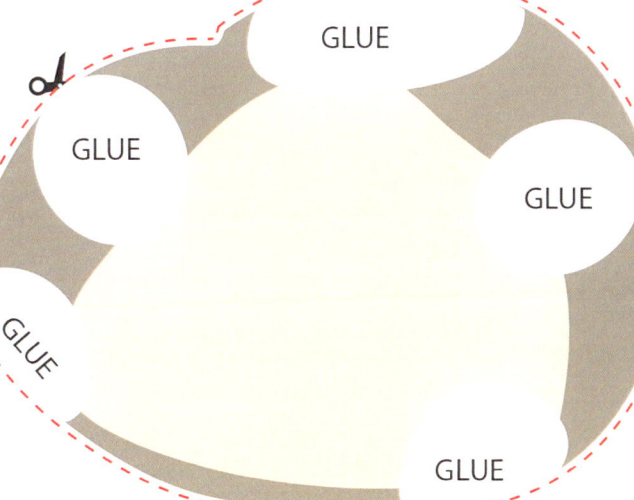

Visit us at:
www.adventuresofscubajack.com

www.ingramcontent.com/pod-product-compliance
Lightning Source LLC
Chambersburg PA
CBRC090749020526
44118CB00031B/244